A New Song

Elizabeth Sprehe

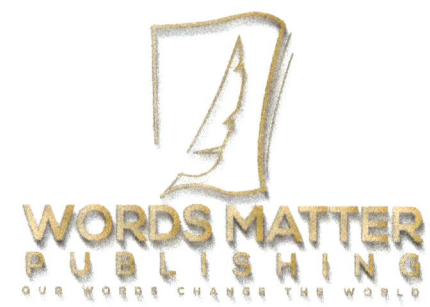

© 2018 by Elizabeth Sprehe. All rights reserved.

Words Matter Publishing
P.O. Box 531
Salem, Il 62881
www.wordsmatterpublishing.com

No part of this publication may be reproduced, stored in a retrieval system, or transmitted in any way by any means—electronic, mechanical, photocopy, recording, or otherwise—without the prior permission of the copyright holder, except as provided by USA copyright law.

ISBN 13: 978-1-947072-53-4
ISBN 10: 1-947072-53-6

Library of Congress Catalog Card Number: 2018936787

I dedicate this book to my sisters, they fed me, housed me, took me to Church regularly and showed me how to live this life.

Table of Contents

A Little Rain	10
A Quiet Cry of Suffering	12
A True Believer	14
Advent Prayer	16
Arrogant	18
Assurance	20
Astray	22
Believe	24
Blindly	26
Change	28
Choices	30
Crown of Life	32
Don't Worry	34
Eternal Love	36
Extra Portion	38
Filthy Rags	40
Forgiveness	42

A New Song

Full Control	44
Give Me Strength	46
Give To Me	48
God Is In Control	50
Grant Me Faith	52
He Came To Me	54
He Leads Me	56
Help Me	58
His Good Time	60
His People	62
Hold My Hand	64
How Long	66
I Can Do All Things	68
I'm Trusting You	70
In Your Image	72
Instrument of Love	74
IT SEEMS WE CAN'T GO ON	76
JUST LET GO	78
JUST LIKE A MOTHER	80
KING WITHOUT A CROWN	82
LEAD ME	84
LORD WHEN YOU SPEAK	86

A New Song

LOVE ONE ANOTHER	88
MY ALL	90
MY SHEPHERD	92
MY SONG	94
NEVER BE DISCOURAGED	96
NEVER LET ME STRAY	98
ON THIS ROAD	100
ONE MOMENT OF PLEASURE	102
ONE WISH	104
OUR CROSS	106
OUR NEEDS	108
PROMISE	110
QUIET TIMES	112
REFLECTION	114
SHOW ME DIRECTION	116
STORMS OF LIFE	118
TAKE MY HAND	120
TEACH ME	122
THANKS	124
THAT STILL SMALL VOICE	126
THE BEGINNING	128
THE COVENANT	130

THE CRIB AND CROSS	132
THE EASY WAY	134
THE FORGIVING FATHER	136
THE FUTURE HOLDS NO TERRORS	138
THE HEAVENLY CITY	140
THE KEEPER	142
THE QUESTIONS OF A YOUNG MAN	144
THE RAINBOW MAKER	146
THE REASON	148
THE SAME OLD STORY	150
THE STRANGER	152
THE STRUGGLE	154
THE TILLER	156
THE UNION	158
THERE IS A TIME	160
THIS I KNOW	162
THIS NARROW ROAD	164
THROUGH THE FIRE	166
TO GOD ALONE BE THE GLORY	168
TO LOVE	170
TRUE HAPPINESS	174
TRUST	176

A New Song

WHAT DO THEY SEE	178
WHAT VOICE DO YOU LISTEN TO	180
WHAT'S AHEAD	182
WHEN I AWAKE EACH DAY	184
WHEN I'M IN DOUBT	186
WHEN WE SUFFER ON THIS EARTH	188
WHERE WOULD I BE	190
WHICH WAY YOU GO	192
WHY DO I CRY	194
WOULD YOU	196
WRONG OR RIGHT	198
YEARNING	200
YOU ARE BLESSED	202
YOUR GOODNESS	204
YOUR PRESENCE	206
YOUR TASK	208
YOUR WAY	210
YOUR WORD	212
YOU'RE NOT ALONE	214
YOU'VE BEEN MY GOD	216
About the Author	218

A Little Rain

A New Song

When a little rain falls

Just thank the Lord above

He may be sending blessings

Along with drops of love

Behind the clouds of darkness

A ray of light will shine

The goodness of His mercy

Inside you'll surely find.

And I will make them and the places round about my hill a blessing; and I will cause the shower to come down in his season; there shall be showers of blessing. **Ezekiel 34:26**

A Quiet Cry of Suffering

A New Song

No one that day was waiting
No one to hold His hand
As he went through the bitterness
As He fulfilled God's plan.

Just disbelieving empty stares
Sad eyes that overflowed
No one could feel His loneliness
No one that day could know.

The sad soul-piercing longing eyes
Full of pain and agony
When He endured that awful cross
Bore the shame of sin for me.

The smitten suffering Savior
Gave out a quiet cry
Gave up the flesh—this Son of God
He suffered, and He died.

He is despised and rejected of men; a man of sorrows, and acquainted with grief: and we hid as it were *our* faces from him; he was despised, and we esteemed him not. **Isaiah 53:3w**

A True Believer

A New Song

A true believer
Sees Jesus inside
They see the cross
Where He bled and died
They feel the pain
In His side and hand
They hear the words
From the High command

They see Him die
Upon the tree
They know He died
For you and me
They see the tomb
Rolled back that day
They know we'll live
In Heaven someday.

Then saith he to Thomas, Reach hither thy finger, and behold my hands; and reach hither thy hand, and thrust it into my side: and be not faithless, but believing. John 20:27

A New Song

Prepare our hearts at this advent time
As your birthday, we await
Remove old anger, pride, and sin
The hurt and scars of hate
Lord give us strength to look to Thee
As we start each day anew
To do our best increase our faith
And put our trust in you.

And the apostles said unto the Lord, Increase our faith.

Luke 17:5

A New Song

Somedays I am so arrogant,

I think I've got something no one can get;

I act like I've done some great thing

To deserve this peace only, you can bring.

I do not know the reason why

You chose me, for my sins to die;

But Lord, I'll praise you forever more,

Your Holy Name I'll love and adore.

For by grace are ye saved through faith; and that not of yourselves: it is the gift of God: Not of works, lest any man should boast. For we are his workmanship, created in Christ Jesus unto good works, which God hath before ordained that we should walk in them. **Ephesians 2:8-10**

A New Song

You love me, Lord, this I know
I read your Word, it tells me so.
You made me, and I know you care
My burdens you help me bear.
And when I slip, you love me still
Your presence I can always feel.

Let us draw near with a true heart in full assurance of faith, having our hearts sprinkled from an evil conscience, and our bodies washed with pure water. **Hebrews 10:22**

A New Song

When I am feeling low and my day comes to an end,

My thoughts are in an awful state, I cannot find a friend.

I long to find an end to all this restlessness,

Could it be all my fault and my own carelessness?

Perhaps I've looked too long in wrong places, Lord

I know I've gone astray, I need to hear your Word.

You loved me long ago when I was very young,

Could you still love me after all that I have done?

For ye were as sheep going astray; but are now returned unto the Shepherd and Bishop of your souls.
1 Peter 2:25

A New Song

I can't believe I said that word
I can't believe I failed again
I can't believe I was so bad
I can't believe those were my sins.
I can't believe you died for me
I can't believe you care
Help me believe—increase my faith
My cross I'll gladly bear.

And straightway the father of the child cried out, and said with tears, Lord, I believe; help thou mine unbelief. **Mark 9:24**

Blindly

A New Song

I wonder why I blindly go
Into my day so leisurely.
I'm sometimes selfish, lazy and cross
I think I'll get by so easily.
When I'm alone, I realize what I've done
I ponder all my deeds.

I realize I've failed again,
This brings me to my knees.
If only I'd take the time
To ask the Lord for guidance,
He's always there to lead my way,
The Bible gives me assurance.

The eyes of your understanding being enlightened; that ye may know what is the hope of his calling, and what the riches of the glory of his inheritance in the saints, And what is the exceeding greatness of his power to us-ward who believe, according to the working of his mighty power... **Ephesians 1:18-19**

A New Song

Change is so vital
In order, to grow
It comes on so slowly
But somehow, we know
When changes occur
And we seem at a loss
We can't even reason
Or figure the cost
We always look forward
Once changes take place
And lean on our Lord
For His guidance and grace

But grow in grace, and in the knowledge of our Lord and Saviour Jesus Christ. To him be glory both now and for ever. Amen.

2 Peter 3:18

A New Song

It seems like in this life we have a choice to make

To do what's right or wrong, which road we're going to take

To go along with all the crowd and live just any way

To never care and never love, and live just for today

Or we can choose the narrow road and try to do what's right

To love our neighbor and our God and walk within His light.

I call heaven and earth to record this day against you, that I have set before you life and death, blessing and cursing: therefore choose life, that both thou and thy seed may live: **Deuteronomy 30:19**

When we suffer on this earth, we suffer not in vain

The Lord sends sunshine and blue skies after all the rain.

He tells us to draw near through the suffering and the pain

That's when we learn to lean on Him, our crown of life to gain.

Blessed is the man that endureth temptation: for when he is tried, he shall receive the crown of life, which the Lord hath promised to them that love him. **James 1:12**

A New Song

Don't worry about a thing, it's sometimes hard, it's true

But the Bible says that's what we need not do.

Instead just pray, tell God your needs, and say thanks for His reply.

He'll hear your prayer and do what's best, and peace He'll multiply.

Be anxious for nothing, but in everything by prayer and supplication with thanksgiving let your requests be made known to God. **Philippians 4:6**

A New Song

The lilt of secret-shared laughter
A tenderness in your voice
A heart that flutters with each word
A soul without a choice.

A radiance words cannot describe
Of stars shining in your eyes
The answer to your lonely days
A reply to desperate cries.

The journey of a life together
Heedless of all time and space

The cherished joy of endless days
Incandescent on your face.
A quiet and gentle understanding
As two souls mate for life
Together to share the laughter
Together to share the strife.

Two beings meant for each other
United by God above
Embraced with whispered devotion
And blessed with eternal love.

Be ye not unequally yoked together with unbelievers: for what fellowship hath righteousness with unrighteousness? and what communion hath light with darkness? **2 Corinthians 6:14**

A New Song

Lord send an extra portion of your love and grace today

I know that you can hear me, send something more I pray

I need to feel your goodness with each step that I take

To know forgiveness of my sins each moment I'm awake.

Moreover I have given to thee one portion above thy brethren, which I took out of the hand of the Amorite with my sword and with my bow. **Genesis 48:22**

Filthy Rags

A New Song

I go around from day to day	Your goodness and self-righteousness
On guard each moment with all I say	Will never gain eternal bliss
I do the good that I can do	Old dirty filthy rags are they
To prove to those my love is true	And cannot take your sins away
I see this shadow in the mirror	You must believe in My Dear Son
It asks the face, why are you here?	He is the way—the Only One.

But we are all as an unclean thing, and all our righteousnesses are as filthy rags; and we all do fade as a leaf; and our iniquities, like the wind, have taken us away. **Isaiah 64:6**

Forgiveness

A New Song

Forgive me, Lord, when I'm unkind,
Forget and leave someone behind;
Forgive me when a word I've said
Should cause someone to feel some dread;
Forgive me when I think of me
And I should only think of Thee.

For thy name's sake, O LORD, pardon mine iniquity; for it is great. **Psalm 25:11**

A New Song

When I let God have full control

He gives life meaning He makes me whole

He takes each care, my worries cease

He fills my days and gives me peace.

Thou wilt keep him in perfect peace, whose mind is stayed on thee: because he trusteth in thee.
Isaiah 26:3

A New Song

Give me the strength to carry on when all my strength is gone.

Give me hope to look ahead when everything goes wrong.

Help me to never doubt your goodness each and every day

Even through the darkness, I know your love will find a way.

Thou hast turned for me my mourning into dancing: thou hast put off my sackcloth, and girded me with gladness; **Psalm 30:11**

A New Song

Give me a voice to sing your praise
Give me a light to show the way
Give me hope when I am down
Give me love to spread around.
Give me strength to carry on
Give me patience when things go wrong
Give me understanding and peace today
Give me wisdom to find your way.

If any of you lack wisdom, let him ask of God, that giveth to all men liberally, and upbraideth not; and it shall be given him. **James 1:5**

A New Song

Staring eyes in disbelief
Unable to comprehend
Minds racing and ears unhearing
Of this world, is this the end?

The sky turns gray
And overhead a dust is covering o'er
A stately structure so strong and tall
A structure that is no more.

People running, people leaping
A wild pandemonial state
People watching—people praying
Not knowing their future—their fate.

An evil menacing presence
Invading our homes and land
The Anti-Christ rears its ugly head
And wields his destructive hand.

Lives changed and altered forever
By this demonic foe
The depth and reasons unfathomed
Why? In this world, we'll never know.

Life here is precious, life here is short
But God is in control
The outcome's in His Mighty Hands
The future not for us to know.

Say among the heathen that the LORD reigneth: the world also shall be established that it shall not be moved: he shall judge the people righteously. **Psalm 96:10**

Grant Me Faith

A New Song

When I feel so low down
And the end I cannot see
When no one here I find
Who really cares for me
When days and nights are long
I cannot find a friend

When no one understands
The song inside won't end
When my heart cries out, please
Just trust believe in me
Grant me faith, Dear Lord
To only trust in Thee.

What time I am afraid, I will trust in thee.
Psalm 56:3

A New Song

I was a lost and wretched soul, then Jesus came to me

He cleansed and made me whole, from bondage he set free

He came when I was lost and low when I was full of doubt

He cleansed my heart and soul, made me pure within, without

I'll never know why He chose me, why He came into my heart

When He came He set me free, I pray He'll ne'er depart.

For the Son of man is come to seek and to save that which was lost. **Luke 19:10**

He leads me through swift waters

Through valleys or despair

When all around are gloom and pain

And men don't show they care

He leads me through temptation

When saying no seems wrong

And those around me all say yes

I feel I don't belong

He leads me when I doubt His love

When I doubt salvation and grace

He leads me and will lead me

'Till someday I see His face.

He maketh me to lie down in green pastures: he leadeth me beside the still waters. **Psalm 23:2**

A New Song

Help me Lord, today;
I am weak, can't see your way.
Help me to look ahead,
I'll follow where I'm led
Just help me when I fall,
You are my God—my all in all.

Then came she and worshipped him, saying, Lord, help me. **Matthew 15:25**

Why do we want our way and want it right now

When we wait on God, He shows us when and how

In His good time, He tells which path to take

If only we ask for help, mistakes we may not make.

For my thoughts are not your thoughts, neither are your ways my ways, saith the LORD.
Isaiah 55:8

A New Song

I love this land where we are free,
To worship our God above,
He protects us each and every day
And guides us with His love.
At times it seems we stray too far
And He turns His face away,
But then we hear His promise again
And take the time to pray.
He says He'll bless His people
And forever He will be.
Our Savior and Redeemer
With Him, we'll love eternally.

If my people, which are called by my name, shall humble themselves, and pray, and seek my face, and turn from their wicked ways; then will I hear from heaven, and will forgive their sin, and will heal their land. **2 Chronicles 7:14**

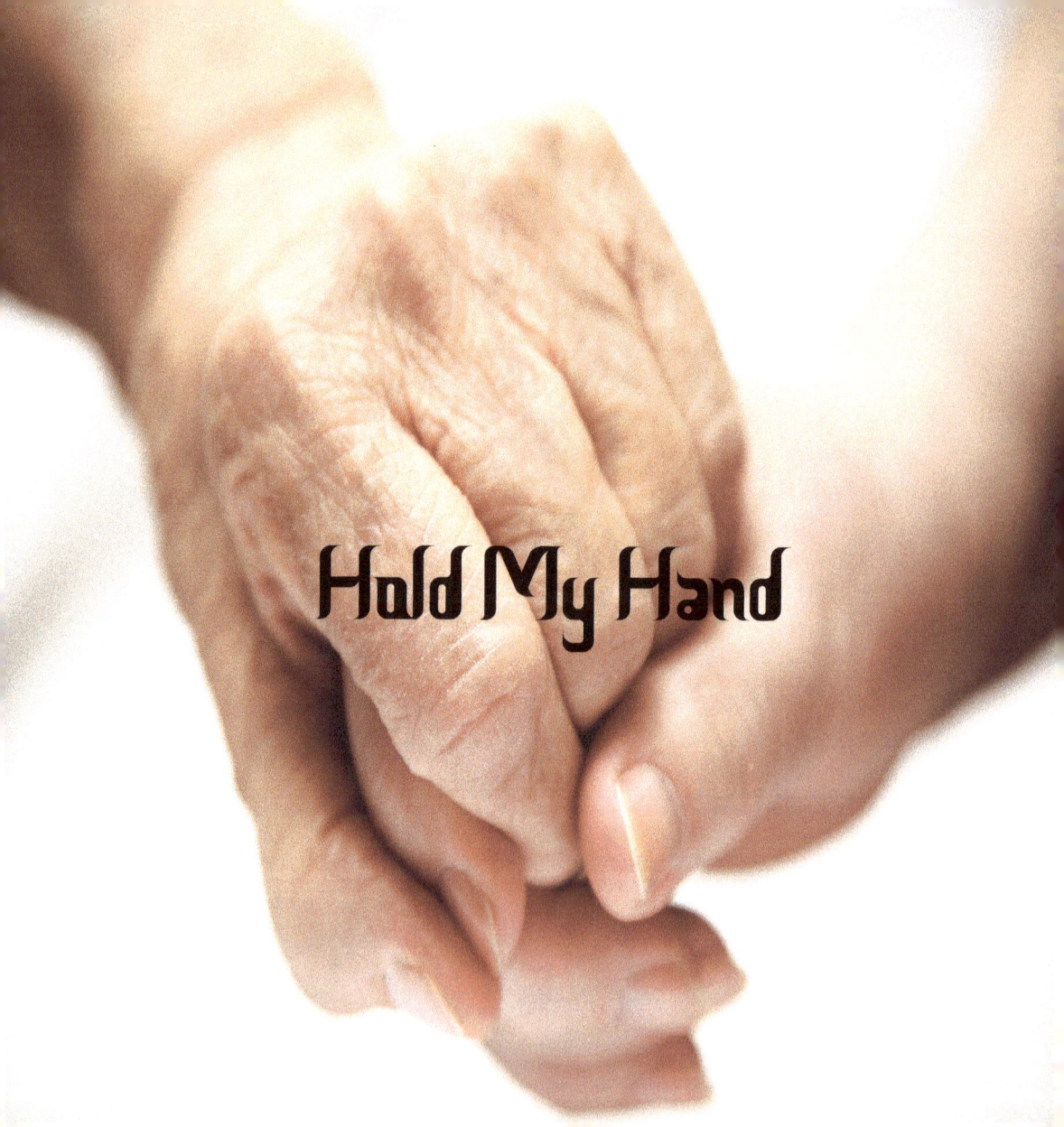

A New Song

When I'm afraid
And need help to stand
Lord guard my heart
And hold my hand.

While I wander here
In this lonely land
Lord guard my soul
And hold my hand.

When those nearby
Don't understand
Lord guard my mind
And hold my hand.

When on that shore
At last, I stand
I know you'll be there
To hold my hand.

Nevertheless I am continually with thee: thou hast holden me by my right hand. **Psalm 73:23**

A New Song

Sometimes we wonder why
Some days we even ask
"Why does this go on
How long will it last?"
Nothing endures forever
Just as in the past
Whether it's good or whether it's bad
Remember, "This too shall pass."

O LORD, how long shall I cry, and thou wilt not hear! even cry out unto thee of violence, and thou wilt not save! **Habakkuk 1:2**

I Can Do All Things

A New Song

I know that I can do all things
Through Jesus Christ my Lord,
I have no need for boundaries
When living in accord.
It is the Lord who gives me strength
To carry on each day,
He'll be my friend, I'll praise His name
For now and time alway.

I can do all things through Christ which strengtheneth me. **Philippians 4:13**

Upon the tree you died for me, you died that I might live.

You bore my sins upon yourself, you said, "Father, please forgive."

They cursed and spat at you, it must have hurt you so

The pain you felt from those angry men, I'm sure I'll never know.

I know at times I hurt you too, by unkind words I say

Forgive me, Lord, I'm trusting you to take my sins away.

Then said Jesus, Father, forgive them; for they know not what they do. **Luke 23:34**

A New Song

I am content with who I am, I would not care to be

Just like some others that I know, some people that I see

I sin each day and don't live right, at times I fear the end

But then I read your Holy Word and know Your Son did send.

So, help me Lord to live each day, content with all you give

You made me in your image, someday with you, I'll live.

For whom he did foreknow, he also did predestinate to be conformed to the image of his Son, that he might be the firstborn among many brethren. **Romans 8:29**

Instrument of Love

A New Song

Thank you, Lord for making me,
Although I'm full of sin.
Thank you, your blood has made
Me whole—without, within.
Thank you for the peace of mind
You giveth every day.
Make me your instrument of love
To help others find the way.

Neither yield ye your members as instruments of unrighteousness unto sin: but yield yourselves unto God, as those that are alive from the dead, and your members as instruments of righteousness unto God. **Romans 6:13**

A New Song

God Heals the Pain

It seems we can't go on
When we lose someone so dear
The pain we cannot ease
Understand why they're not here
We fear our heart will break
And the tears we cannot hide
We look for someone near
In whom we can confide
Each day we search and search
For this one who now has fled
Small comfort do we find
In words sincerely said
But God does heal the pain
As He sends His peace and love
And He grants us sound assurance
Of His mansions up above.

Behold, I will bring it health and cure, and I will cure them, and will reveal unto them the abundance of peace and truth.

Jeremiah 33:6

A New Song

If I was there, I'd hold your hand
To let you know, He understands
If we could talk maybe then you'd see
Why all of this just has to be.
We are God's children and in His care
And so I offer you this prayer
So just let go—let faith abide
He'll see you through, he'll be your guide.

And the Lord direct your hearts into the love of God, and into the patient waiting for Christ. **2 Thessalonians 3:5**

A New Song

Just like a mother cares for her child
My Jesus cares for me.
He feeds my soul, He gives me hope
And sets my Spirit free.
He helps me walk this lonely road
He's my Savior and my friend.
He'll stay beside me all the way
Until my days shall end.

As one whom his mother comforteth, so will I comfort you; and ye shall be comforted in Jerusalem. **Isaiah 66:13**

KING WITHOUT A CROWN

A New Song

The snow was like a blanket, the stars shone bright above
The hay was soft and warm, the stall was filled with love
The babe lay there a-sleeping, a smile upon His face
His birth proclaimed to those around, He'd save the human race.
When Mary spoke to Joseph, the animals stood still
The shepherds came to worship, they traveled o'er many a hill
The heavens suddenly opened, a host of angels came down
To praise the King of Glory, this King without a crown
No other birth in history has turned men's hearts around
As this lowly birth in Bethlehem of this King without a crown.

Glory to God in the highest, and on earth peace, good will toward men. **Luke 2:14**

LEAD ME

A New Song

Lead me on the narrow way,
Keep my feet from straying.
Help me to hear your voice,
To obey what you are saying.
Direct my thoughts and be near me,
Whatever I may do.
Increase my faith and be my friend,
My companion who is true.

Lead me, O LORD, in thy righteousness because of mine enemies; make thy way straight before my face. **Psalm 5:8**

A New Song

The words I hear You speak go deep inside my soul

They penetrate my being, take root and start to grow.

It's when I nurture them and ponder each word from you

They give me strength to carry on, they give me hope anew.

My sheep hear my voice, and I know them, and they follow me: **John 10:27**

A New Song

Love is patient, love is kind

Love waits its turn and doesn't mind

Love does not envy, it is not proud

Love is so quiet, not very loud.

Love doesn't get angry, it is not rude

Love is so gentle, does not act crude.

Love keeps no record of wrong or right

Love doesn't enjoy a feud or a fight

Love always protects, always hopes, always trusts.

Love never fails, it endures, it must!

A new commandment I give unto you, That ye love one another; as I have loved you, that ye also love one another. **John 13:34**

A New Song

In a little church a long time ago

I gave my all to Christ, at least I thought was so.

But I only gave a portion, I withheld a great big part,

It seemed I was not ready to give Him all my heart.

And as the years went by I tried to work things out

I only messed them up, of this, there was no doubt.

My mind was in a constant whirl, my body racked with pain,

I knew I could not go on, I knew I had to change.

I met the Lord one night, in an unexpected place,

It was a little frightening as if we were face to face.

He told me never ever to fear, He'd be there if I'd fall,

But he wanted all I had, He wanted my all and all.

I had to give Him everything, all that I possessed

For this, He promised eternal life, His peace, and happiness.

So likewise, whosoever he be of you that forsaketh not all that he hath, he cannot be my disciple. **Luke 14:33**

A New Song

The Lord of Lords is my shepherd

He leads me

He guides me

He restores me

What more could I want?

Beside gentle waters

Through deaths dark door

Before my enemies

He comforts me.

My soul is His

I am His namesake

He prepares a place for me

And I shall dwell with Him

Forever and ever in my home

In Glory. Amen.

A Psalm of David. The LORD is my shepherd; I shall not want. **Psalm 23:1**

A New Song

You fill my soul with gladness
Take away all sadness
And give me a song to sing.
You turned my pain and sorrow
Into bright tomorrows
This is the joy you bring.

May I ever praise your name
Bring glory, honor, fame
And be your child forever.
So as time and days go on
I'll lean upon you strong
Do not forsake me ever.

And he hath put a new song in my mouth, even praise unto our God: many shall see it, and fear, and shall trust in the LORD. **Psalm 40:3**

There's really nothing we need know
Or should try to understand
If we refuse to be discouraged
And trust God's guiding hand.

So just take heart and meet each moment
With faith in God's great love
Aware that every day of life
Is controlled by Him above.

And never dread tomorrow
Or what the future brings
Just pray for strength and courage
And trust God in all things.

And never be discouraged
Be patient and just wait
For God never comes too early
And He never comes too late.

"Cast thy burden upon the Lord And He shall sustain thee." **Psalms 55:22**

NEVER LET ME STRAY

A New Song

Sometimes I feel so hollow inside
Like nothing left, no love no pride
I go around feeling glum and forlorn
I ask myself why I was born
My days repeat at a steady pace
Its like I'm only marching in place.
I almost loose my way, your lead,
Then suddenly the light again I see
It may be a word or a song I hear
To let me know you care, you're near
Lord never let me stray too far
Stay by my side each moment, each hour.

With my whole heart have I sought thee: O let me not wander from thy commandments.

Psalm 119:10

A New Song

I walk along this narrow road, I sometimes lose my way.

I do not always take the time or even stop to pray.

I get off step, I go astray and the road I cannot see.

I listen to other people instead of trusting Thee.

Then dimly I see the way, the course opens up to me

Why was I so blind, the road I couldn't see?

I hear you speak, I feel your touch I know that you are near.

It's when I listen, and I pray, you're voice inside I hear.

And thine ears shall hear a word behind thee, saying, This is the way, walk ye in it, when ye turn to the right hand, and when ye turn to the left.
Isaiah 30:21

A New Song

One moment of pleasure
One half-second of bliss
One slight indiscretion
One moral amiss.

No one will be looking
No one here will know
No one will see me
Just one wild-oat to sow.

It won't really matter
It will hurt no one
Its only experiment
Its only for fun.

Its just for my pleasure
Nothing lost nothing gained
One moment of pleasure
And a lifetime of pain.

Choosing rather to suffer affliction with the people of God, than to enjoy the pleasures of sin for a season; **Hebrews 11:25**

A New Song

If I could have, but one wish,
Then I would wish for you
That your days would be many
And your troubles all be few.
That the Dear Lord send His blessing
To earth from heaven above.
May He keep you safe and care for you
And enfold you with His love.

Beloved, I wish above all things that thou mayest prosper and be in health, even as thy soul prospereth. **3 John 1:2**

OUR CROSS

The sin and shame we carry, because of foolish ways
Brings pain and grief and sorrow, despair both night and day
The load gets oh so heavy, we stumble, and we fall
We give God a small part, but He wants our very all
Its when we give Him all we have, no matter what the loss
He's there our sins to forgive, He's there to bear our cross.

Looking unto Jesus the author and finisher of our faith; who for the joy that was set before him endured the cross, despising the shame, and is set down at the right hand of the throne of God.
Hebrews 12:2

A New Song

We all have needs to be fulfilled, somedays they are so strong

We first need love to give and receive and know that we belong

And then understanding of what we do when we are right or wrong

To create in our own little world as we write or sing a song.

You need a place where you feel secure, a place just for you

And to seek adventure, maybe dare to go and do what you should not do

To know somewhere, there's a God who cares that's bigger than you and me

To know and feel Him deep within although others cannot see.

Casting all your care upon him; for he careth for you. **1 Peter 5:7**

A New Song

Your promise Lord of heaven is what I felt today

In the sky, I saw your rainbow so very far away.

I felt some tiny raindrops fall upon my face,

They made a little puddle in this dry and barren place.

I saw the earth and sky renewed by God's tender love,

I felt your promise in my soul, your power from above.

I do set my bow in the cloud, and it shall be for a token of a covenant between me and the earth.
Genesis 9:13

A New Song

I love the quiet times when I'm alone
And I know we're in tune.
That's when I stop to hear your voice
Its then we can commune.
Its not out there on a busy street
Or in a noisy crowd.
But only when I'm so quiet,
Then, Lord, You speak so loud.

Be still, and know that I am God: I will be exalted among the heathen, I will be exalted in the earth.
Psalm 46:10

A New Song

Somedays I feel like a teen age girl
All silly and giddy and in a whirl
So full of pep and energy
Then suddenly this reflection I see.
Could that lady really be me?
The hair is gray—there's wrinkles I see!
The years have passed so swiftly it seems
At times its almost like a dream.
I couldn't have made it, Lord its true
I couldn't have made it without you.

For now we see through a glass, darkly; but then face to face: now I know in part; but then shall I know even as also I am known.
1 Corinthians 13:12

SHOW ME DIRECTION

A New Song

Dear Lord please tell me where I'm at right now
I feel so lost alone. I need to grow, but how?
Why do I feel so silent as if I'm standing still
Show me direction, your presence Lord let me feel.

Thou wilt shew me the path of life: in thy presence is fulness of joy; at thy right hand there are pleasures for evermore.
Psalm 16:11

A New Song

Sometimes when the storms of life toss us to and fro

We wonder how will it end—which way should we go?

Should I do this or choose that way or maybe just give in

No one seems to understand, we cannot find a friend.

But when we turn to God and put our trust in Him,

He's always there to calm the storm, the victory to win.

What manner of man is this, that even the winds and the sea obey him? **Matthew 8:27**

TAKE MY HAND

A New Song

Dear Jesus take my hand today,
Can't see your plan, can't find a way.
I feel so weak, forlorn and low,
I just can't tell which way to go.
I need your hand to guide my way
To show me what to do and say.

Show me thy ways, O LORD; teach me thy paths.
Psalm 25:4

A New Song

Teach me Lord your ways
To treasure all my days.
Teach me to love you more
Your holy name adore.
Teach me to help some one
To look inside and see your Son
Teach me to live for Thee
And to forget me.

Lead me in thy truth, and teach me: for thou art the God of my salvation; on thee do I wait all the day. **Psalm 25:5**

A New Song

I thank the Lord for daily bread,
I thank the Lord for life;
I thank the Lord for everything,
I thank the Lord for strife.
It's through the winter and the fall
I sometimes lose my way.
But thank you, Lord, you give me spring,
This great and glorious day.

In every thing give thanks: for this is the will of God in Christ Jesus concerning you.
                                1 Thessalonians 5:18

A New Song

Is it loud and is it clear
Does it bring you down
Or does it bring you cheer?
We all have voices deep inside—
Voices that we hear
Listen for the voice of God—
That still small voice so dear.

And after the earthquake a fire; but the LORD was not in the fire: and after the fire a still small voice. **1 Kings 19:12**

A New Song

This life began so perfect,
When life did first begin
It became corrupt and lonely
Because of doubt and sin
When man took over all things
And did them in his own way
He tried to be as great as God
Who made the night and day
But then the Maker of all things
Had mercy and love for man
He sent to earth His Only Son
He fulfilled His special plan.

Therefore as by the offence of one judgment came upon all men to condemnation; even so by the righteousness of one the free gift came upon all men unto justification of life. For as by one man's disobedience many were made sinners, so by the obedience of one shall many be made righteous. Moreover the law entered, that the offence might abound. But where sin abounded, grace did much more abound: That as sin hath reigned unto death, even so might grace reign through righteousness unto eternal life by Jesus Christ our Lord. **Romans 5:18-21**

A New Song

He spoke to Abram long ago and made a promise that day

He said he'd lead a nation and bless him on his way

He told him then to leave that land, and with him, He would go

The man, of course, was full of doubt but the Lord his way did show

At times he did some dreadful deeds, but his God was always true

He loved and forgave Abraham that same way He loves you.

Down through the years, He's been so kind our sins all to forgive

He's kept His covenant of old, with Him someday we'll live.

And I will establish my covenant between me and thee and thy seed after thee in their generations for an everlasting covenant, to be a God unto thee, and to thy seed after thee. And I will give unto thee, and to thy seed after thee, the land wherein thou art a stranger, all the land of Canaan, for an everlasting possession; and I will be their God. **Genesis 17:7-8**

FROM CRIB TO CROSS

THE CRIB AND CROSS

A New Song

In the shadow of the crib,
A lonely cross does stand
No shepherds here or wise men near
To hold dear Mary's hand
She remembers when they worshipped Him
As in the crib, He lay
Others mocked and laughed at Him
On the cross that dreadful day
Was He unkind or did He do
Some wrong to deserve such agony
They took her babe the King of Kings
And nailed Him to a tree
In her heart, she knew the crib and cross
Were God's special plan
His Son was born, He bled and died
To save the soul of man.

But Mary kept all these things, and pondered them in her heart. **Luke 2:19**

A New Song

To always choose the easy way, to live and just skim by

To think you're always cheated and never ask yourself why

To exert no effort great or small or take even a small part

To always choose the easy way is to always cheat the heart.

And from the days of John the Baptist until now the kingdom of heaven suffereth violence, and the violent take it by force. **Matthew 11:12**

A New Song

"I want my share, I want my part."
The young man said—soon to depart.
"The world's out there, 'n I want to see
Adventure and fun are waiting for me."
"My eldest brother, your first born son
Will care for you, he'll be the one."
The father listened, understanding was he
He knew very soon his son would flee.
He let him go, and he prayed to God
Lord keep him safe on the roads he trods.
The young man squandered, he lost his share
No one was there, no one to care.
He wanted his freedom, the world to see
Adventure and fun were now agony.
"I sleep among the swine at night
Eat crumbs from tables, find no delight."
"My father's servants live better than me
I'll return at once, very soon I'll flee."
God said, "Go home, your father awaits
For you he yearns, for you, he aches."
The father was watching, he saw from afar
A young man was coming—his soul was ajar.
He remembered his gait, and his heart leapt inside
His hands were trembling, his eyes-how they cried.
The son, the wanderer, had come back to his home
No more needing adventure, no more needing to roam.
Like our Heavenly Father with arms open wide
He welcomes us home with Him to abide.

For this my son was dead, and is alive again; he was lost, and is found. And they began to be merry. **Luke 15:24**

A New Song

The Future Holds No Terrors

The future holds no fears
The Lamb, His sheep, will feed
Will wipe away our tears
We will not be despondent
But courageous and will wait
For God never comes to early
And He never comes too late.

And God shall wipe away all tears from their eyes; and there shall be no more death, neither sorrow, nor crying, neither shall there be any more pain: for the former things are passed away.

Revelation 21:4

A New Song

That heavenly city prepared for me—
Prepared by God's own hand.
I long to go—I long to see—
Before my Lord to stand.
I want to see my mother dear
All those who've gone before.
To smile and hold their hand
As I walk thru the door.
So please don't weep—don't cry for me.
You see, I'm better off than thee.

But ye are come unto mount Sion, and unto the city of the living God, the heavenly Jerusalem, and to an innumerable company of angels...
Hebrews 12:22

THE KEEPER

A New Song

The town looked cold and dark as they rode in late that night

The maiden was young and weary, they had made a long, long flight

The keeper could not find a room in his tiny, crowded inn

But he was a kind and gentle man so to his stable he did send

He gave them a lamp and some clear dry hay to make for them a bed

Could he have known that the King of Kings on this straw would lay His head?

As he bid farewell and turned to go, he saw a blinding light

Somehow, he knew in his heart and soul the Messiah would come this night

He was the keeper of the inn, he asked the Lord to stay

The Lord's the Keeper of your heart do not turn Him away.

The LORD is thy keeper: the LORD is thy shade upon thy right hand. **Psalm 121:5**

THE QUESTIONS OF A YOUNG MAN

A New Song

One day a young man came to me, asking
Where do your poems come from
Do you think of them as you go along
Do you write for fame or fun?

Do you sit around and meditate
Think about poems night and day
Do you wonder what will come to you
Wonder what next you will say?

And do you sit n' try to figure things out
Like what's going on in the world
Who keeps us on your journey here
What keeps life in a whirl?

Then tell me about the universe
Who rules our lives each day
Who do you thank for everything
Each day t' whom you pray?

And then he asked 'bout the evil we see
'bout this cruelty to man
Is this the way it's meant to be
Can this be part of God's plan?

So, for a while, I pondered these things
And I prayed "What shall I say?"
Lord give me courage to answer him
Help me to show Your way.

So, I went to see this kind young man
And we talked for many-an-hour
We talked about God's love and grace
We talked about His power.

How He can take a sinful man
A person like you and me
With His love and grace and forgiveness of sin
How He can set us free.

How He formed the world and universe
And He still has full control
How He gave His promise in His Word
To the saints so long ago.

If man will only follow Him
And let Him lead the way
We'll live with Him forever
There will be but glorious days.

And as for me and the thoughts that I think
And the poetry that I write
I praise my God and give Him thanks
Every day and every night.

But sanctify the Lord God in your hearts: and be ready always to give an answer to every man that asketh you a reason of the hope that is in you with meekness and fear: **1 Peter 3:15**

A New Song

When days are bright and sunny
I oft don't think of You
I think I've done some great big things
To make my skies all blue.

But when the gray mists gather
And the storm clouds touch my soul
I toss, I fret and worry
I wonder which way to go.

I try alone to work things out
And I wrestle on and on
Until no longer I can go on
I know I cannot win.

At last, I give God all my cares
And He grants me peace to see
The sun comes out and overhead
The rainbow shines for me.

As the appearance of the bow that is in the cloud in the day of rain, so was the appearance of the brightness round about. This was the appearance of the likeness of the glory of the LORD. And when I saw it, I fell upon my face, and I heard a voice of one that spake. **Ezekiel 1:28**

A New Song

We get so busy this time of year

With work and home to tend

We even wonder and sometimes ask

Will I finish? Will it end?

We take on all these little tasks

And somehow, they seem to grow

We may forget the reason why

But deep down we really know.

Its this special time so dear to us

This advent we await

The coming of our Lord and King

In our hearts we celebrate.

For we have not followed cunningly devised fables, when we made known unto you the power and coming of our Lord Jesus Christ, but were eyewitnesses of his majesty.
2 Peter 1:16

THE SAME OLD STORY

A New Song

Its just the same old story
The one you know so well
For years it's been repeated
This story that I tell.
The prophets knew about it
So very long ago
The people did believe it
And it began to grow
They started out proclaiming
Christ Jesus and His love
The Holy Spirit led them
And descended like a dove

It's just the same old story
'Bout Jesus' love for you and me
How He came to earth to bear our sins
How He came to set us free
To some, the story may sound old
But to me, it's always new
It's about forgiveness and His grace.
And God's love for me and you.

Therefore if any man be in Christ, he is a new creature: old things are passed away; behold, all things are become new. **2 Corinthians 5:17**

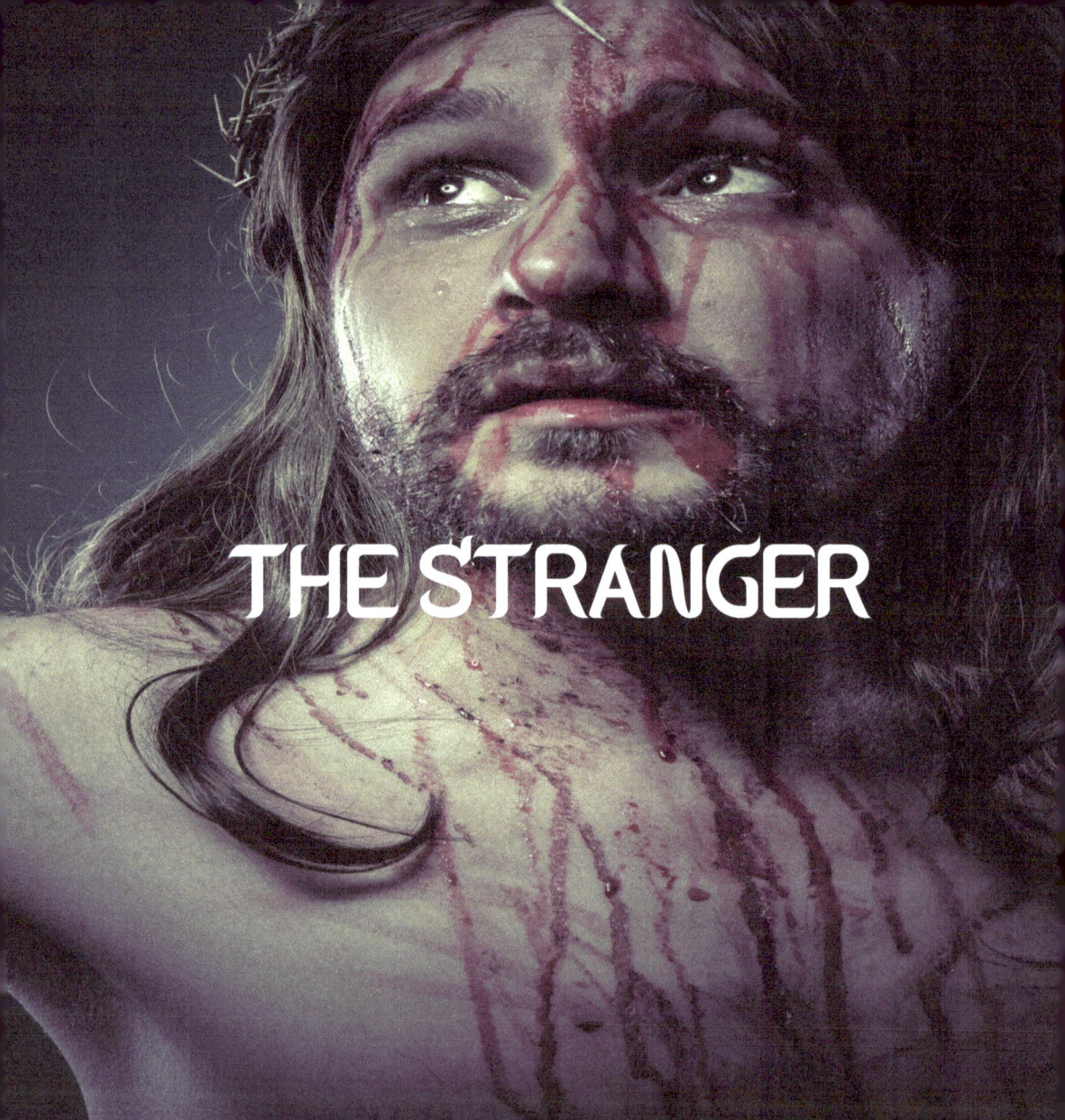

A New Song

Who was that man?

His eyes just pierce my soul

Who was that man?

He spoke so clear and bold

They say He came

To turn men's hearts around

He shed His blood

On the cross and on the ground

He loved them still

As He hung on that lonely tree

Who was that man?

Did He die there for me?

And a stranger will they not follow, but will flee from him: for they know not the voice of strangers. This parable spake Jesus unto them: but they understood not what things they were which he spake unto them. **John 10:5-6**

THE STRUGGLE

A New Song

We all have days and days it seems
When nothing's going right,
The struggle with our selves,
There's always such a fight;
Should I do this or go that way?
I cannot always know,
Tell me Lord, just who I am
Show me which way to go.

For our struggle is not against flesh and blood, but against the rulers, against the powers, against the world forces of this darkness, against the spiritual forces of wickedness in the heavenly places.
Ephesians 6:12

A New Song

What thoughts man thinks, what dreams he dreams
As he works and tills the land.
Does he wish for fame and youth once more
And things not in God's plan.

Does he long for places far away
Excitement—dancing girls
Who leave his pockets empty
His mind all in a whirl.

Would he care to toil in a tiny place
Or a factory large and tall
Or push a button, punch a clock
Or perhaps not toil at all.

Could he behold God's precious world
The spacious sky-rich soil
And know the goodness of His love
Our Lord, the giver of all.

And could he hear the Spirit's voice
When a storm's 'bout to appear
To know in each and everything
He cares—He's always near.

To know the thrill, the hope
And beauty, the wonder of the spring
Each man should be a tiller
To know the joy it brings.

but he will say, 'I am not a prophet; I am a tiller of the ground, for a man sold me as a slave in my youth.' Zechariah 13:5

A New Song

A marriage made in heaven
Ordained by God above
A union of our children
United by their love
To trust and truly care
And forgive along the way
To take it oh so slowly
And learn to live each day
And though at times their strength will wane
And skies may turn to gray
If only they will trust in God
He'll surely light the way
To never grow discouraged
Or dread a fresh new dawn
But pray for strength and patience
And courage to carry on
And so, the maker of this union
The gracious God above
Has looked down in His mercy
And bestowed His precious love

And did not he make one? Yet had he the residue of the spirit. And wherefore one? That he might seek a godly seed. Therefore take heed to your spirit, and let none deal treacherously against the wife of his youth. **Malachi 2:15**

A New Song

For everything, there is a season

For all things, there is a reason~

There is a time to laugh and a time to cry

A time to live and a time to die

A time to gather and a time to sow

A time to come together and a time to go

A time to work and a time to play

A time to be quiet and a time to say

A time to lose and a time to win

A time to begin and a time to end!

To every thing there is a season, and a time to every purpose under the heaven: **Ecclesiastes 3:1**

A New Song

"I know not what the day may bring,
If sorrow, joy, or tears,
But I know Jesus will be there
To share my hopes and fears.

I know He'll watch, through dark the way;
He never tires or sleeps,
But ceaselessly where'er I be
A tender vigil keeps.

I do not know what He has planned;
His hand I cannot trace.
But daily I can hear Him say,
'Sufficient is My grace.'
And 'In the time of trouble, call
On Me, I'll see you through.'
He often sends me joy through pain,
He'll do the same for you.

It's good to know that He is near
By night as well as day,
To share our losses and our gains
And guide us all the way."

And he said unto me, My grace is sufficient for thee: for my strength is made perfect in weakness. Most gladly therefore will I rather glory in my infirmities, that the power of Christ may rest upon me. **2 Corinthians 12:9**

A New Song

Teach me, Lord, to lean on you
And ever keep my love so true
To not grow weary of the load
And stay right on this narrow road.

Because strait is the gate, and narrow is the way, which leadeth unto life, and few there be that find it. **Matthew 7:14**

A New Song

Lord when you lead me through the fire

I feel Your presence remain

I see the flames my heart then knows

I'll be no more the same.

You mold me as the flames grow near

And the heat grows more intense

My spirits wane, my eyes grow dim

My mind has no defense.

It's when You reach into my soul

And quench the fires that burn

I find new meaning for my life

New strength to carry on.

If any man's work shall be burned, he shall suffer loss: but he himself shall be saved; yet so as by fire.
1 Corinthians 3:15

A New Song

I remember so clearly that very first morn
When I was oh so small
I didn't know just what to expect
I didn't know much at all.

I marched right in—I was afraid
Wasn't sure what I was to do
Was I supposed to stand or sit
There wasn't one face that I knew.

We sang some songs, we learned to read
It happened so long ago
I don't recall how it all came about
But I know it surely was so.

They strove to shape young people
Into fine young women and men
The teachers devoted their lives to us
And showed us how to begin.

We read about God's mercy and grace
When I was very small
I didn't know the depth of God's love
I didn't know much at all.

That place was just a little place
Not many in the school
They taught reading, writing, arithmetic
They taught the golden rule.

The years—they've gone so swiftly
Back when I was small
Didn't know how to live this life
I didn't know much at all.

But one thing I earned at that little school
When I was oh so small
No matter which road I travel
No matter how often I fall.

God's love will always see me through
He'll be there when I call
He shows me how to live this life
He is my God—my all.

He takes me back where I started from
He takes me back to school
He shows me how to live each day
He teaches the golden rule.

So, to God alone be the glory
He's been here through it all
He is the greatest teacher
The greatest of them all.

Now unto the King eternal, immortal, invisible, the only wise God, be honour and glory for ever and ever. Amen. **1 Timothy 1:17**

A New Song

My mind screams loudly inside of me—

Why are you living? What will you be?

Are you doing anything great?

And for all things, you wait and wait!

It seems you cannot find a friend—

Is this all? Are you near the end?

And then a deeper voice in me,

(Answers softly)

Can't you feel, can't you see

It is my heart and its reply

For you, I came; for you, I died.

My Lord speaks to my heart and soul—

I put you here to love and grow.

We know that we have passed out of death into life, because we love the brethren. He who does not love abides in death. **1 John 3:14**

TOMORROW

TODAY

YESTERDAY

A New Song

Cherish this day

It passes fast.

Look for tomorrow

It holds great hope

Forget yesterday

It is history.

Jesus Christ the same yesterday, and today, and forever. **Hebrews 13:8**

A New Song

So many people complain these days
They work so hard for so little pay
They can't be content
With what they possess
They think only money
Brings true happiness
But it can't be bought
And it can't be won
It's given by God
It's free through His Son.

Not that I speak in respect of want: for I have learned, in whatsoever state I am, therewith to be content. **Philippians 4:11**

A New Song

When I put trust in men right here
They sometimes let me down
I hang my head I run and hide
My face wears a sad frown
Do I expect too much from them
More than they can give
Teach me, Lord, to trust in Thee
And learn each day to live.

Put not your trust in princes, nor in the son of man, in whom there is no help. His breath goeth forth, he returneth to his earth; in that very day his thoughts perish. Happy is he that hath the God of Jacob for his help, whose hope is in the LORD his God: **Psalm 146:3-5**

A New Song

Young eyes see my errant behavior
See the things I'd hope they not see
They hear my words my actions see
Eyes look directly back at me

At times I get carried away
Say things that make me not proud
I talk and slander my neighbor
Say abrasive things out loud

I hope they can see my shame
See my pain and agony
See the hurt that I've inflicted
See the person I try to be.

Or perhaps they see a person at peace
See my joy and see my glee
Can they see the love I give
See the love returned to me.

Can they see the hope and longing
See the wisdom that waits for me
See the temptations I can conquer
With Christ's blood who has set me free.

In all things show yourself to be an example of good deeds, with purity in doctrine, dignified. **Titus 2:7**

A New Song

Is it loud and is it clear?

Does it bring you down?

Or does it bring you cheer?

We all have voices deep inside—voices that we hear

Listen for the voice of God—that still small voice so dear.

For he is our God; and we are the people of his pasture, and the sheep of his hand. Today if ye will, hear his voice. **Psalm 95:7**

A New Song

What lies ahead tomorrow
Do you really want to know?
You may have pain and sorrow
Or your cup may overflow
There might be fields of flowers
Or dreary nights and days
Your path could be so rugged
Or smooth along the way
You might just have to travel
Alone, but for awhile
And look and pray to God above
To return that once used smile
So be content to rest in Him
Continue to love and grow
What lies ahead tomorrow?
That's not for us to know.

"So do not worry about tomorrow; for tomorrow will care for itself. Each day has enough trouble of its own. **Matthew 6:34**

A New Song

When I Awake Each Day
And take the time to pray
I thank the Lord above
For His quiet gifts of love.
My day will always be
As great as any you see
My heart will overflow
He's with me wher'er I go.

When I surrendered my all
To you so long ago
I didn't know right then
Which roads I'd have to go
I never knew I'd feel
Such love and joy inside
Or peace and happiness
Could stay and abide
I love this feeling Lord,
This love you gave to me
I'd try to do my best,
So your love, others through me see.

For whether we live, we live unto the Lord; and whether we die, we die unto the Lord: whether we live therefore, or die, we are the Lord's. **Romans 14:8**

A New Song

I may not know where some roads lead
Or why some days I cry, I bleed;
I trust Dear Lord you'll light my way
When I'm in doubt, teach me to pray.

I will therefore that men pray every where, lifting up holy hands, without wrath and doubting. **1 Timothy 2:8**

When we suffer on this earth,

We suffer not in vain

The Lord sends sunshine and blue skies,

After all the rain.

He tells us to draw near

Through suffering and the pain

That's when we learn to lean on him,

Our crown of life to gain.

And if children, then heirs; heirs of God, and joint-heirs with Christ; if so be that we suffer with him, that we may be also glorified together.
Romans 8:17

WHERE WOULD I BE

A New Song

Where would I be without the Lord beside me every day,
I would not have contentment, and I doubt that I would pray.
I could not find the sun even on a cloudless day,
I know I'd not be here—I'd be someplace far away.

I thank you, Lord, for making me—although I'm full of sin
I thank you, your blood has made me whole—without, within
I thank you for the peace of mind you giveth every day.
Make me your instrument of love to help others find the way.

Yet for this reason I found mercy, so that in me as the foremost, Jesus Christ might demonstrate His perfect patience as an example for those who would believe in Him for eternal life. **1 Timothy 1:16**

A New Song

My heart is heavy, my spirit low
Please tell me Lord, which way to go;
My friends are gone, they can't be near
I can't talk to those right here-
Am I the one who has gone astray?
I've only trusted your Word to show the way
Don't leave me now, for I must know
Which way my life just has to go.
Give me assurance and hope today
And always remind me to trust and pray.

Let not your heart be troubled: ye believe in God, believe also in me. **John 14:**

WHY DO I CRY

A New Song

When people near,
Don't seem to care
'bout hurts and fears.
How can they know
How can they feel
The pain inside
The pain so real.
If they could go inside
of me
Then they would know
Then they could see
But Lord you know
Just what I feel
The pain and hurt
I know you'll heal.

For we have not an high priest which cannot be touched with the feeling of our infirmities; but was in all points tempted like as we are, yet without sin. **Hebrews 4:15**

WOULD YOU

A New Song

He did not travel o'er many lands

Or high office ever hold

He was not named as royalty

But of mansions, we are told

He was the King of glory

From Heaven to earth came down

He had no jewels or finery

Or even an earthly crown

He came to earth as a little child

Born in a lowly stall

He gave up all He had

He came to save us all

Would you have loved so deep and true

For someone like you and me

Or would you give up all you have

To die on a lonely tree?

Let this mind be in you, which was also in Christ Jesus: Who, being in the form of God, thought it not robbery to be equal with God: But made himself of no reputation, and took upon him the form of a servant, and was made in the likeness of men: And being found in fashion as a man, he humbled himself, and became obedient unto death, even the death of the cross.
Philippians 2:5-8

A New Song

Each of us has to live
Our very own way
What is right for you
Who is to say?
What's wrong for me
May be right for you
Or the other way around

Could be true
But there's only one way
To heaven above
Thru forgiveness of sin
And Jesus blood.

Neither is there salvation in any other: for there is none other name under heaven given among men, whereby we must be saved. **Acts 4:12**

A New Song

I yearn to travel and see the world
The wonders of this place
To gaze with long and searching eyes
At this lonely human race
To take the time to make some friends
Along this road, I trod
To find the meaning of my life
To get in touch with God.

Draw nigh to God, and he will draw nigh to you. Cleanse your hands, ye sinners; and purify your hearts, ye double minded. **James 4:8**

A New Song

You are so blessed to have this child for such a few short years,

He'll bring joy to your heart and also bring you tears;

He'll watch you both all the while--all that you do and say.

You'll be the ones he'll lean upon, the ones to point the way.

So, stick by the Lord, stay by His side

He's always there; He'll be your guide.

Train up a child in the way he should go: and when he is old, he will not depart from it. **Proverbs 22:6**

A New Song

Its whispered on the wind
And echoed up above
The goodness of Your grace
The vastness of Your love.

Great choirs can raise the strain
Their loud hosannas sing
And symphonies expound
The beauty of everything
But words cannot explain
Your goodness Lord and Your love

Its whispered on the wind
And echoed up above.

Therefore they shall come and sing in the height of Zion, and shall flow together to the goodness of the LORD, for wheat, and for wine, and for oil, and for the young of the flock and of the herd: and their soul shall be as a watered garden; and they shall not sorrow any more at all. **Jeremiah 31:12**

YOUR PRESENCE

A New Song

Lord, I need to feel your presence, every minute, every day

I long to know your love, no matter what others say

To feel secure and not give up when storms toss me about

To just believe and keep on going and never ever doubt.

And he arose, and rebuked the wind, and said unto the sea, Peace, be still. And the wind ceased, and there was a great calm. **Mark 4:39**

A New Song

Do the task that lies before you each and every day.

You may not know the rules or even what to say.

Just ask the Lord for direction and for His endurance,

He'll be right there to help you, He'll give you sound assurance.

Commit thy way unto the LORD; trust also in him; and he shall bring it to pass. **Psalm 37:5**

A New Song

You've stood by me
And held my hand
You've pulled me through
And helped me stand.
When dark and long
My nights and days

You were the lamp
You lit the way
And when Your way
I fail to see
Lord help me know
You still guide me.

For as the heavens are higher than the earth, so are my ways higher than your ways, and my thoughts than your thoughts. **Isaiah 55:9**

YOUR WORD

A New Song

I never tire of reading your word
Its' your sweet words inside I've heard,
They always are alive and new
It's a message, Lord, to me from you.

Thy word have I hid in mine heart, that I might not sin against thee. **Psalm 119:11**

YOU'RE NOT ALONE

A New Song

Long ago when I was small, I felt so all alone

I had my life, my family, and a happy home

I asked the Lord why was I here, why was I born? I cried.

As time went by, deep down I heard His reply

You're not alone—I've sent the Holy Spirit

You're not alone—He's by your side

You're not alone—just trust His promise

This is the greatest truth—you're not alone

And the LORD, he it is that doth go before thee; he will be with thee, he will not fail thee, neither forsake thee: fear not, neither be dismayed.
Deuteronomy 31:8

A New Song

You've been with me all the way
You've seen me thru the darkest days
You've held my hand lest I should fall
You've been my God, my All and All.

Thou art my God, and I will praise thee: thou art my God, I will exalt thee. **Psalm 118:28**

About the Author

Writing was a past-time for Elizabeth almost all of her young days. When she was very young, she would simply doodle because she had a hard time expressing her thoughts and feelings. Elizabeth came from a small town in Southern Illinois where people gossiped about everyone else but did not express their own problems. She was the youngest of six children, so naturally, everyone called her the baby.

Living in a small town was quite an experience because there was very little entertainment and interest. The biggest excitement was when the carnival went through town. The town was so small that when the coal mines shut down, many people left town. Babies were birthed at home by midwives in their own home. Elizabeth was delivered by a doctor who charged fifty dollars a visit. The older girls were very helpful by cleaning the house, airing the bedding outside each spring and helping with the laundry on the wringer washer. Elizabeth was not old enough to help with the chores but she and her sister Mary helped by carrying the coal into the house. Anywhere Mary went Elizabeth followed. Many of the townspeople could not figure out who was who, so they called them Mary Beth. Soon the name Beth stayed with Elizabeth. Each day when Mary walked to school, she would walk with her friend and Beth would just tag along. Mary and Elizabeth thought everyone lived like they did, little did they know things were going to change.

In 1942 their mother became very ill. She was in a lot of pain, and she was going blind. She was taken to the hospital in Missouri where she received radiation treatments that did not help her and soon she was sent home where she died in 1942.

Later Mary and Elizabeth went to live with the older sisters until they graduated from high school. They got jobs and started living in an apartment where they declared they would be "career girls"! At the age of 17, Elizabeth got a job with a Communication Company. One day while sitting at her desk she wrote on the pad of paper the words "Who Am I?" which became her first poem. She finally expressed her feelings, and she was no longer called Elizabeth.

www.ingramcontent.com/pod-product-compliance
Lightning Source LLC
Chambersburg PA
CBHW051246110526
44588CB00025B/2899